MIRA

Astonishing Moments & Turning Points

A Collection of Mira(cle)Doodles - Volume 2

Dedicated to M & RL

Doodles #1-31 are drawn based on INKTOBER 2020 prompts
Doodles #32-62 are drawn based on INKTOBER 2021 prompts
Doodles #63-93 are drawn based on INKTOBER 2022 prompts

Disclaimer: The information shared in this book is for educational and informational purposes only and is not intended to be viewed as medical or mental health advice. It is not designed to be a substitute for professional advice from your physician, therapist, attorney, accountant or any other health care practitioner or licensed professional. The Publisher and the Author do not make any guarantees as to the effectiveness of any of the techniques, suggestions, tips, ideas or strategies shared in this book as each situation differs. The Publisher and Author shall neither have liability nor responsibility with respect to any direct or indirect loss or damage caused or alleged by the information shared in this book related to your health, life or business or any other aspect of your situation. It's your responsibility to do your own due diligence and use your own judgment when applying any techniques or situations mentioned in or through this book. Any citations or sources of information from other organizations or websites are not endorsements of the information or content the website or organization provides or recommendations it may make. Please be aware that that any websites or references that were available during publication may not be available in the future.

Publisher: elinap, Vantaa, Finland
Design & illustrations: elinap
ISBN 978-952-67473-7-8 (Paperback)
ISBN 978-952-67473-8-5 (Hardcover)

Spending time with Mira and her friends helps us
reveal the ways the ego disrupts our peace of mind.
Every doodle in this collection is an invitation to return back to Love
time and time again by listening to your heart:

Use each doodle as a little exercise to find ways in which it could illustrate aspects of your life: maybe the ego has been stirring your thoughts up lately (#2), or perhaps it has set a trap on your path that you can now decide to avoid (#18). What are the pearls of wisdom you can find in every experience (#66), and what could a fairytale ending look like for you (#86)? The answers will be unique to you. The doodles have symbols that allow for your own interpretations and insights to surface.

These doodles were drawn daily in October of 2020, 2021 and 2022, inspired by the one-word prompts of Jake Parker's INKTOBER challenge. They are presented in the same order as the prompts were given, with five short stories in between.

My hope is that Mira and her friends inspire
shifts in how you view your life and
make choosing Love feel
easy & fun!

Meet the Characters

MIRA is an ever-curious, joyful inner child who loves to follow her heart and doesn't stop, even when the ego butts in.

MIRA'S HEART represents inner wisdom. The heart symbolizes the Love that we are—a Love that is all-encompassing and all-accepting. She knows our birthright is Love, Joy and Ease. The heart never leaves Mira even if she loses sight of it. Love will stick around like the Sun: Clouds may hide the sun, but it still shines.

MIRA'S FRIEND, SANDY, represents all other people and our interactions with others. She reflects Love and loyalty back to Mira or mirrors the ego, depending on which voice Mira chooses to listen to.

A LIZARD symbolizes the ego, representing moments when we try to play it safe and make decisions from our primary brain (also called the lizard brain).

It's helpful to remember that the ego always speaks first and loudest in its attempts to lead us away from Love. The ego offers replacements for Love that always leave us wanting for more, as nothing is ever enough for the ego.

Other Symbols Used in This Book

STARS symbolize miracles, which are shifts in perception according to *A Course in Miracles*. Shifts happen when we question the world that the ego shows us and start to wonder if there is another way of looking at our situation.

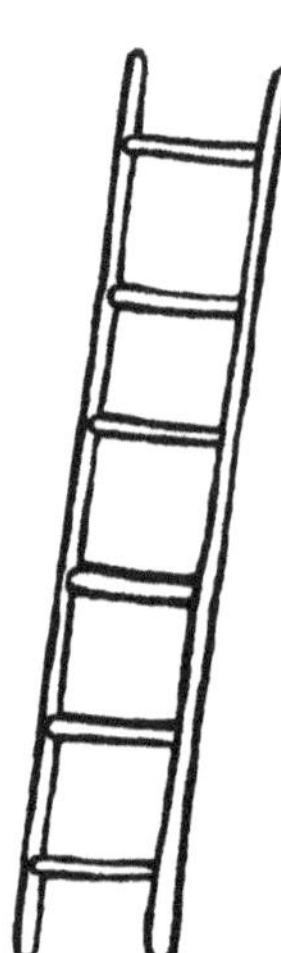

A LADDER represents the times in life when we awaken to the reality that we are unhappy and desire a change.

A THOUGHT BUBBLE symbolizes thoughts and dreams.

When drawn as balloons on a string, the thoughts are being brought into our awareness.

A PATH represents our life unfolding with every step and every decision we make.

A PEN represents the way we express our creativity, whether it's through drawing, writing, dancing, cooking, gardening etc.

ALL THE SYMBOLS are drawn to help us move forward, towards more light & Love.

So, what are we waiting for? Let's turn the page and begin!

The ego feeds on compliments, but Love needs none.
Love knows happiness is an inside job.

P.S. I misread this prompt (it was WISP).
Isn't it interesting how creativity can arise from mistakes too?!

Sometimes the ego just takes up all the space. It's almost impossible to hear the whispers from the heart when the ego gets so bulky.

Is abundance like
a switch to turn on or
a channel to tune into?

What if it's both?
You are the switch, and you are the channel—abundance flows
from within. You are enough.

We might think we are holding a sword in our hand, but instead it's hovering above our head…

Every time we're tempted to be angry at someone we are choosing between freedom and pain.

Hurting them hurts us, but thanking them sets us free, and the sword disappears.

Imagine all the things I could do if I was as small as a mouse!
Oh, but what if you were the size of a dinosaur?
You are great just the way you are!

They say we live in a post-truth society now; it's
the intensity of the message that matters.

Can you recognize the bells and whistles of the ego?

Look past the intensity and keep listening to
the gentle whispers of your heart.

Even if it's loud and fancy it doesn't make it more important!

Can you see the world
from your thoughts?

When choosing Love, you need to throw away
the thoughts you thought with the ego.

The heart KNOWS that all is well at all times.

Yuck, stop it! That's disgusting, hope sucks.
Sorry...
I can't. It's just the way I am.

What would you do if you knew you couldn't fail, even if you fell?

Let Love catch you.

Is there no end to these?
If you're willing to follow, I can get us out of here in no time!

The ego has solutions for all
the problems it has created.

At the edge of our comfort zone,
we can find the final challenge…

How do we get past the guard who thinks it
has our best interests at hand?

At the speed of Love they traveled.

I have the power to choose peace...
No matter how intense the storm.

When we recognize the ego's trap, we can step out of it—with Love.

Note that this can go on forever when we are too dizzy to keep count!

What would the fish say?

An awakened mind is listening.

The ego's promises have kept us waiting for so long.
There's always something missing like an odd ingredient or
time for the stew to cook. What would Love do?

The contracts we sign with the ego are "not set in stone".

The ego asks us to dig in pursuit to find something more,
a reason, an explanation, a treasure of any kind—but the
deeper we dig the darker it gets. It's harder to see.

However, when we dig with Love, we build foundations
and expand from there.

Just keep digging. I'm sure you'll hit your goal pretty soon!
I'm shoveling as fast as I can!

What happens next—after you notice that
it's the ego you've been running with?

Have you been playing hide and seek with miracles lately?
Just let them find you!

Let your pen dance to the music of your soul.

Floating in the infinite possibilities of the universe.

The ego always looks for an external solution,
just like it looks for an external enemy too.

When you notice an ominous thought, reach out
to your heart and let the thought go.

Even though the ego may have helped us crawl to the finish line, deep in our heart we know we were already there, every step of the way.

One breath at a time, Mira started climbing out,
leaving the darkness behind.

A Suit or a Vessel?

The body is like a suit that the ego uses to cover the truth.

But this feels wrong...
Just zip it up!

But Love isn't defeated so easily!

The body becomes a vessel for spreading
more Love into the world.

Get curious and pay attention.
Love will tell you how to do it!

Psst... Listen to me!
I quit

There's a loving solution for every knot on our path.

When a message from power animals seems threatening, please listen closely—there's a loving intention at the core of every message.

Challenges and struggles are gratifying for the ego,
and worth all the sweat and tears.

The key to happiness though, is realizing
there is no wall built between you and Love.

I. Can. Do. This.
That's the spirit!
But...
I thought we'd use the door...

No matter how powerful a fan is,
it won't blow away the thoughts you cling to.

Let's stop falling into the ego's lies of one more try and
one more chance of pursuing happiness.

Facing the Scary Stuff in Our Lives

One day I took the bull by the horns
and faced the scary stuff in my life.

Of course, the scary stuff had a big message for me…

My willingness to ask was enough, and the answers started pouring in.
In essence though, there was just one answer.

It was unbelievably simple like all
great answers tend to be.

Aw, I'm so sorry, I didn't mean to abandon you!

We are Love,
and everything else is
a cry for Love.

Every struggle is just a reminder to
find our way back to peace.

- THE END -

When we are ready to take a leap of faith, all we need to do is
to stop trying to convince the ego about it and just do it!

Just fake it until you make it!
I. Can't. Fake. It. Much. Longer...

We are in this together.
Let's pick up each other.

Either let the thought go or look for ways to see it differently.

Ask for Help

Are you stuck, Mira?
Are you trying to do it
alone again?

Look around... do you see
anyone you could help?

See, maybe you are not
that stuck after all!

By helping
others...
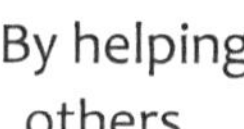

...your own needs become
crystal clear.
You now know how to get going!

You just need to do one simple thing:
Ask your heart.

She knows
exactly what
your next step
would be.

Help flows freely,
naturally!

You get to receive it too!

You just need to ask.

- THE END -

Don't let the ego hold you back when you've got something to celebrate. Shout it from the rooftops!

And keep dancing no matter what the ego says!

When was the last time when you were fully present in the moment?

When the Ego Takes the Wheel

Our inner compass works even from the passenger seat.
Miracles are still there waiting!

The ego always
explains the outcome in its favor,
and we are so used to its views on happiness
that it's hard to notice we got in trouble again...

- THE END -

It's never too late to question...

Love's idea of happiness is infinite joy that keeps on giving, growing and forever expanding.

Are you going to let the ego paint the next thought for you?

Mira is getting stronger in saying 'No' to the ego no matter how much added cuteness there is. Let's follow her example and do the same.

Love welcomes us back with open arms at
any moment… again and again.

Let them go! That's the only wise thing to do with
the thoughts the ego has painted for us.

The ego's biggest fear is that it'll become extinct…

Ha, and here's another attempt to paint Mira's thought!
The ego is quick indeed!

When the ego connects the dots, it builds complex
structures and adds layers that cover up the truth.
They are fascinating and take forever to explore.

When Love connects the dots, it's so simple that
it peels off all the layers the ego built.
Love fills us with peace and understanding.

Ta-Dah!
Love is all you need.

When light enters darkness, it's no longer dark.

My inner child goes wild with joy in crisp weather,
when there are patches of ice to jump on!
How about you—what fills you with joy?

But... It feels fake...
Shush now!
Just take it!

The ego is persistent, but Mira is starting to pay attention now!
Hooray!

This is the only risk worth taking—see you on the other side!

What if gargoyles could have a day of rest from looking so scary?

When we keep choosing Love,
we start to shine so bright that the ego
no longer feels welcome.

A bat once almost hit me in the face at full speed!
Had I become invisible for a while or was this a wake-up call?

Look for a deeper meaning—a pearl of wisdom
within every experience you go through.

It's just a tiny spark of hope now but it's got all the power to...
...to burst into flames of inspiration!

Not even in its wildest dreams would the ego
believe that less is better than more. Never.
But it often is.

The ego had lured Mira into a detour once again, until she remembered to listen to her heart. She was happy to notice that her detours were getting shorter and shorter each time.
It's easier to remember!

When we meet each other at the soul level,
it's a match every single time—with anyone!

We don't need to build a beautiful nest for Love.
Love is unconditional and here to stay!
But it's also okay if you do. Love doesn't Judge.

The ego can get very crabby when we try to expand
and reach towards our next miracle.

When it's time to gain some perspective, step back and look at the bigger picture. It's quite beautiful, isn't it?

...But her heart knows better, Mira already did forget by preparing for future failures. You don't need to prepare for the future when you live in the now. Every moment is a new beginning.

We have so much Love to give!
Keep loving. Keep giving. Be kind.
It always comes back to you, multiplied.

I come to you with empty hands and an open mind.
And I'm happy to fill them up for you!

Your strength comes from within, you've already got all you need.

Put all your ducks in a row—with Love.

The ego always finds a way to justify judgment. Don't listen to it.

NO!
Jump!

With the ego I'm barely making it.
That's when I'm creatively stuck, life doesn't flow,
and I never feel like I have enough or do enough.
I *am* never enough.

With Love, abundance of everything I yearn to have—creativity,
joy, and even more Love and happiness—is the default.
Abundance flows freely.

I think the choice is pretty clear:
Jump and join the miraculous flow of life and Love
with joy!

When was the last time you truly listened to your inner child?
It looks like she has waited for some time…

When we take the first timid steps to follow
our heart, the ego calls it a bluff.
Let's prove the ego wrong...

When we nurture others at the cost of our own wellbeing,
we might need to hang a warning sign at some point…

If it was this obvious, would we keep allowing
the ego to rob us of our happiness?
In which sneaky ways is the ego stealing
your happiness from you right now?

This prompt sucks…

A Fairytale Ending

The ego yearns for a fairytale ending,
but Love is happy in the moment.

It doesn't prevent the ego from trying, though...

With her decision to choose Love instead,
she lived happily ever after.

- THE END -

Oh no... indeed, what would a day feel like if
we gave our full attention to the ego?
Perhaps like most of our days, eh?

"True wisdom is being able to say, 'It is what it is' with a smile of celebratory wonder on your face."

Eric Micha'el Leventhal

This is where I found you, so this is where I'll stay. I never want to lose you again!
Well, you know, I'll go with you wherever you go! I always do.

Uh-oh, am I
in trouble?

But where are they hiding?
You're funny.
I'm right here, all you need is to ask.
Backpack filled with crystals, card decks, self-help books & online courses, life coach on speed dial...
Mira's hunt for miracles isn't going as well as she planned...

Look, here's a fresh batch of seeds for loving thoughts!

What kind of thoughts are you cultivating in your mind?

Plant the seeds of happiness today,
and let them grow and flourish in
every moment!

DOODLING MIRACLES
- INSPIRING JOY & REFLECTION -

Mira(cle)Doodles are illustrations from a spiritual path, born from a need to question the ego's ways and to follow the heart no matter what comes your way.

Inspired by inner musings about life, they simplify and explain life's struggles and spiritual challenges with a loving twist. They show how it's possible to choose Love and be at peace in any moment.

The doodles help you connect with your own inner wisdom and inspire you to expand into a deeper understanding of life and Love.

ABOUT THE AUTHOR & ILLUSTRATOR

Elina Puohiniemi, aka elinap, is an artist, life coach and
the creator of the Mira(cle)Doodles series.

She has been illustrating her spiritual path with doodles
since 2010. For the past nine years, she has explored
life with her symbolic doodle character, Mira, in her
(almost) daily doodling.

She lives in Finland with her husband, their
two teenage sons and a poodle.

ALSO IN THE MIRA SERIES

MIRA Glimpses of Life & Whispers from the Heart (2022)

OTHER TITLES BY ELINAP

THE FOUR PHASES OF CREATIVITY
A Path to Unleashing the Natural Flow of Your Creativity (2021)

MORE DOODLES AT

WWW.DOODLINGMIRACLES.COM